60 DAY FITNESS PLAN

60 DAY FITNESS PLAN

An individual exercise
program for men and
women of all ages

p

This is a Parragon Publishing Book
First published in 2004

Parragon Publishing
Queen Street House
4 Queen Street
Bath BA1 1HE, UK

Produced by The Bridgewater Book Company Ltd

Main photography by Ian Parsons

ISBN: 1–40542–647–0

Printed in China

contents

why get in shape?

Active living and a healthy diet are fundamental to everyone's general health, vitality and quality

of life, but the imbalanced nature of modern-day living tends to encourage us into a poor diet and

a sedentary lifestyle, in which we have little motivation to be physically active.

REASONS TO GET IN SHAPE

❖ improved feeling of well-being
❖ increased strength and flexibility
❖ more stamina
❖ reduced stress levels
❖ lowered blood pressure
❖ reduced cholesterol levels and a healthier heart
❖ weight loss
❖ better quality of sleep and alleviation of insomnia
❖ slowing down of the aging process
❖ lower risk of late-onset diabetes
❖ relief of aches and pains
❖ increased levels of energy
❖ enhanced ability to recover from illness or injury
❖ better posture
❖ improved muscle tone
❖ improved health

There are many reasons for us to get in shape and stay active and one of the main arguments is, possibly, because that is what we were designed to do. Humans are animals and until very recently in our history our existence was centered around some kind of physical effort. Indeed, our very survival depended on it—our ability to be active allowed us to catch food, run away from enemies, climb trees and cross rivers. Nowadays, with our reliance on technology and mechanization, we no longer need to be physically active to survive in the outside world, yet our essential needs have not changed

TIME TO BE FIT

Nowadays, many people seem to take better care of their cars and their computers than they do of their bodies or their health. A common complaint seems to be that people don't have the time either to exercise or to pay attention to their diet—and yet they do seem to have the time to be ill! Surely those of us who want busy, full lives should focus on the fact that we don't have time to be unfit and unhealthy!

and in order to function effectively and efficiently our entire system—physical, mental and spiritual—requires daily activity. Also, it is not only our muscles that benefit from movement: our organs, glands and systems (circulation, digestion, respiration) become much more efficient when we are active and in good shape.

Even in the short term, committing ourselves to a program of regular exercise can drastically improve our fitness levels. It can—surprisingly quickly—tone and strengthen our muscles; increase our vitality; reduce insomnia; focus our minds and improve our ability to think clearly; regulate our appetite and encourage us to eat healthily; improve our circulation, breathing, posture, strength, flexibility and stamina; and lift our mood and reduce stress. In the long term, our muscles become more toned, we reduce our risk of disease, improve the way our bodies look and feel, and slow down the aging process.

It is not necessary to join a gym or spend a fortune on fitness – your exercise program can be followed very easily in your own home.

A BALANCING ACT

Nowadays we spend so much time "in our heads", and not being active, that exercise is essential in order to bring us back into our bodies and re-establish balance between the physical and mental in our lives.

LETTING GO

When we are active and in shape it can be much easier to find the motivation to let go of bad habits and addictions such as smoking.

1. I have all the energy I need...

a. always

b. sometimes

c. never

2. I am within ... pounds of my ideal weight.

a. 10

b. 10–20

c. over 20

3. I make time for exercise...

a. every day

b. when I can

c. rarely

4. I get restless when I'm inactive...

a. always

b. sometimes

c. never

5. I'm happy with my physical condition...

a. agree

b. somewhat agree

c. disagree

6. My job keeps me active...

a. always

b. occasionally

c. never

7. I participate in a recreational activity...

a. at least once a week

b. at least once a month

c. rarely

8. I do aerobic exercise...

a. 2 or more times a week

b. occasionally

c. almost never

9. I let things like bad weather or
inconvenience prevent me from exercising...

a. never

b. sometimes

c. often

10. I can walk a mile in...

a. 15 minutes

b. 15–20 minutes

c. more than 20 minutes

11. I have family members or housemates
who keep me active at home...

a. always

b. sometimes

c. never

12. My job, hobbies or home activities
require lifting or stooping...

a. often

b. sometimes

c. rarely

13. I drive even when I have an opportunity
to walk...

a. rarely

b. occasionally

c. always

14. I park as closely as I can to my destination
and use elevators or escalators...

a. never

b. sometimes

c. always

15. I enjoy physical activity...

a. always

b. sometimes

c. never

16. I stretch before and after exercise...

a. always

b. sometimes

c. never

17. I have the appropriate shoes, clothing
and equipment to exercise regularly...

a. always

b. sometimes

c. never

WHAT'S YOUR SCORE?

Give yourself 3 points for each "a" answer,
2 points for "b" and 1 point for "c".

40 POINTS OR MORE, you're living
a healthy, active lifestyle at a high
fitness level.

21–39 POINTS, there's room to improve your
lifestyle and raise your fitness level. A more
active fitness plan is definitely
recommended.

20 POINTS AND BELOW, your lifestyle is
sedentary and you have a low fitness level.
Inactivity and lack of fitness increase your
chance of developing many life-threatening
diseases. It's definitely time to adopt a
healthier, more active lifestyle.

HOW HEALTHY IS YOUR DIET?

1. What do you usually eat for breakfast?
a. healthy breakfast (e.g. cereal, oatmeal, toast and fruit)
b. just juice or fruit
c. high-fat breakfast/don't eat breakfast

2. How many full meals do you eat a day?
a. 3
b. 2
c. 1

3. How often do you eat eggs, cheese and cream?
a. fewer than 3 times a week
b. 3–4 times a week
c. every day

4. How much water do you drink in a day?
a. 8 or more glasses
b. 5–8 glasses
c. fewer than 4 glasses

5. Do you eat the fat on meat?
a. rarely or never
b. often
c. always

6. How often do you eat lean meat and fish or vegetarian alternatives?
a. at least once a day
b. 3–4 times a week
c. less than twice a week

7. How often do you eat fresh fruit and vegetables or drink fresh juices?
a. at least 5 times a day
b. at least once a day
c. around 4 times a week

8. How often to you eat potato chips, cakes or chocolate?
a. rarely or never
b. sometimes
c. regularly

9. How often do you eat wholegrain foods?
a. regularly
b. sometimes
c. never

10. How often do you drink alcohol?
a. less than twice a week
b. 3–4 times a week
c. every day

WHAT'S YOUR SCORE?

Give yourself 3 points for each "a" answer, 2 points for "b" and 1 point for "c".

24 POINTS OR MORE, you're eating a healthy balanced diet.

13–23 POINTS, there's room to improve your diet. A more balanced diet with regular meals would greatly increase your feeling of well-being and general energy levels.

12 POINTS AND BELOW, your eating habits are not doing you any favors. You would greatly benefit from revamping your diet completely and eating nutritious, balanced meals. Try making gradual changes to your diet (such as cutting out sugary snacks and eating fruit or nuts instead, or cutting down on the amount of fried food you consume and broiling or steaming instead), rather than dramatically altering your diet all at once.

choosing a fitness regime

A healthy, fit body is one that is strong, flexible, supple and stable, with good muscle control. The best exercise program for any individual is a balanced system that covers all these areas, encouraging improved levels of all-around fitness while also being enjoyable to perform.

TYPES OF EXERCISE

Many people, even those who already like exercising, tend to favor one type of exercise over another—some people prefer the gym, running or lifting weights (which develop strength and stamina and build muscle), while others are much more interested in quieter, gentler methods, such as yoga, stretching or Pilates (which help develop flexibility and good muscle control—although they too can greatly improve strength).

Do you want to exercise? You will be much more inclined to stick to your routine if you are absolutely certain that it's what you want to do. If you have decided to embark on an exercise program simply to please someone else, you are much less likely to succeed.

When deciding upon an overall fitness plan it is essential that you take your own preferences into consideration, while also bearing in mind the necessity of creating a balanced routine. If you are someone who favors Pilates, yoga or tai chi, for example, make sure that you include at least one or two sessions a week of cardiovascular exercise (such as aerobics, swimming, a dance class or even brisk walking—any exercise that raises your heart rate and makes you sweat a little). On the other hand, if you are a dedicated runner or a gym fanatic, it is imperative that you include some kind of stretching in your program. As well as stretching to warm up and cool down, schedule in two or three 20–30-minute stretching sessions each week, or, if you don't have the motivation to stretch on your own, why not enlist the help of a friend or enroll in a weekly class?

MOTIVATION

It is much easier to stick to an exercise program once you know what your true motivation is and what you are hoping to achieve. What are your reasons for getting in shape? Do you want to lose weight, gain weight, build muscle, tone up, be more active, fit into the clothes you wore two years ago? Once you know your long-term goal, you can work toward it by setting short-term goals.

Also, think about your personality type. Are you someone who prefers to choose one type of exercise and perfect that one technique, or do you get bored easily and would you be happier involving yourself in a range of different activities? Do you enjoy competition and thrive on testing your skills against others, regardless of your current level of ability? Does spending time surrounded by others motivate you, or do you prefer the idea of exercise as a solitary pastime? Is your purpose of being active purely to have fun and find relaxation? Choosing your activities and your approach to them to match your own preferences will make it far easier for you to maintain a long-term fitness plan.

For those fit enough to do it, running combines fresh air, excellent cardiovascular exercise and the opportunity to enjoy time on your own.

When choosing your regime, give yourself easily achievable goals. Instead of simply deciding to "get fit" or "lose ten pounds", focus on goals such as walking a mile, doing 20 minutes stretching, or swimming 10 laps three times a week.

training the body, training the mind

Getting in shape is not simply about exercising our muscles. We stand a much better chance of success and of being able to stick with any program if our minds are involved too. In training or retraining our bodies we also have the opportunity of training our minds.

The chances are that if you're at a stage where you are planning on committing to a new fitness regime, you are thinking about making changes to your life in other ways too—maybe even discovering a new you. Be precise about the things you want to change—make a list of them—determine exactly what your ideals and your dreams are. Perhaps you are feeling under par, unfit and out of condition. Perhaps you are not feeling good about yourself or your body. Well, even so, choose a place to start and work toward realizing your dreams one at a time, step by step. Don't wait until you are feeling fully in shape and toned before you start making little changes—do it now.

JUST SHOW UP

Ninety percent of getting fit and staying in shape is about getting to the gym or actually making sure we do our exercise program. Therefore, it is actually our mind that determines whether or not we are able to stick with our routine and fulfill our intentions.

POSITIVE THINKING

A positive mental attitude is essential to our chances of succeeding in attaining our fitness goals. Think positive at all times. Get into the habit of affirming several times a day: "It is possible" and "Of course I can do it." Say it

EASY TARGETS

Change one thing at a time—nothing will change until you do. Just set yourself the goal of making small, simple changes and you will be amazed at the effect.

out loud, if it helps! A firm mental belief that change is always possible and attainable will get you much further than doubting your own abilities and giving in to a feeling of helplessness.

LISTEN TO YOUR BODY

Learn to listen to your body and avoid pushing yourself too far as you exercise, particularly when you are first starting out. Taking small achievable steps will ultimately produce much better results than pushing yourself too far too quickly, and will allow you to increase gradually your levels of strength, stamina, flexibility and vitality. Focus on doing the exercises correctly, breathing easily and keeping your body in alignment as you work.

EMOTIONAL ENERGY

In order to function at our optimum efficiency—both physically and mentally—there is no doubt that we need to have sufficient nutrition, water, exercise and rest. However, we should remember that around 70 per cent of our energy is purely emotional—the kind that manifests as hope, resilience, passion, fun and enthusiasm. Make sure you both protect and replenish that emotional energy. Staying active and in shape provides a positive step toward achieving this.

Give yourself permission to become a healthier, happier, more vibrant you through creative visualization. Take a few minutes every day to visualize yourself as healthy, happy and overflowing with energy. When you exercise, create an image of yourself doing well and focus on the positive changes that are occurring to your physical and mental well-being as you work out.

Eating healthily, taking regular exercise and spending time in nature helps to balance our emotional energies as well as keeping us physically in shape.

healthy eating

A nutritious and healthy diet is an essential part of any fitness plan. Trying to eat healthily may need a great deal of effort at first, but it is entirely possible to enjoy what you eat and still have a healthy, balanced diet. A personal nutrition diary will help you stay on track (see page 62).

In order for your body to function at its most efficient level, it requires quality fuel to sustain and nourish it. This means that you need to eat plenty of fresh fruit, vegetables and salads, low-fat dairy products, baked or steamed lean meat and fish, soy and tofu, nuts, whole grains and cereals, as well as cutting down on fatty and pan-fried food, white flour, refined sugar, processed food, alcohol and coffee.

Avoid sugary foods because, after the initial boost, they will cause your blood-sugar level to crash, leaving you feeling hungry and depleted. Instead pack some healthy nibbles to take with you when you go to work or to the gym, so that you won't be tempted to snack up on chocolate or potato chips. Choose fresh fruit, dried fruit and nuts, raw vegetables or a glass of fresh juice.

Concentrate on changing your diet gradually rather than making sudden dramatic changes that might result in your feeling "deprived" of those foods that you have become so used to. Choose simple, "real" foods rather than processed or packaged products and focus on all the things that you are able to eat, rather than dwelling on the things that you can't. Replace lunchtime fries with a baked potato and ask for extra vegetables or salad when ordering a sandwich. If you are in need of something sweet, try some frozen yogurt instead of chocolate or ice cream.

WATER

A healthy diet should also include plenty of drinking water, both to keep your body hydrated and to flush toxins from the body. Try to cut down on coffee, tea and sugary drinks—drink a glass of water or a cup of herbal tea instead. And remember, always drink some water after exercising, to replace any that you may have lost while working out.

Choose complex carbohydrates for breakfast (such as muesli) and a little protein (maybe some yogurt) to give you slow, sustained energy throughout the morning.

In the Western world we now consume more (refined) sugar in two weeks than our ancestors consumed (in fruit and other natural forms) in an entire year.

BELOW *Always drink some water after exercising to counteract any dehydration.*

If you are aiming for permanent weight loss, eat healthy, well-balanced meals and snacks in moderate portions, exercise regularly (include cardiovascular exercise, strength training and stretching in your routine) and make sure you get sufficient rest.

LEFT *Plenty of delicious, fresh vegetables are essential when you are eating for fitness.*

EATING FOR FITNESS

DO EAT	EAT ONLY IN MODERATION, OR NOT AT ALL
fresh fruit	refined flour
fresh vegetables, especially leafy green vegetables	sugar, candy, soda and desserts made with sugar
whole grains, wholegrain bread	pan-fried foods
lean meats or fish	full-fat dairy foods
raw, steamed, and baked foods	caffeine and alcohol
fruit spreads made with 100% fruit (no sugar)	fatty meats
skim milk and low-fat cheeses	

getting started

When you are embarking on anything new it can be difficult to know where exactly to begin or how to organize yourself. In starting a new exercise program, be flexible and be prepared to experiment in order to discover what works best for you.

HOW TO EXERCISE

For those of you who have never exercised before, who have only attended occasional classes and are not used to a regular exercise routine, or who have become unfit through not exercising for a while, it can be difficult to know exactly where to start. Frequently, expectations of yourself are set too high and you can become easily disheartened and give up too quickly.

One of the key elements is to go easy on yourself and recognize that in making the decision to commit to a fitness plan, you have already taken a big step. Let go of any preconceived notions of what you "ought" to be able to achieve, and you will be doing yourself an enormous favor. Remember, the only person you need to compare yourself to is

Problem foods that are high in fat, sugar and salt can lead to excessive weight gain and are linked to conditions such as heart disease.

you. Forget those lycra-clad fit young people who appear to be constantly bubbling over with energy. This is your journey—honor it.

Always start your program slowly, at least until you are familiar with the exercises, and remember that any of the exercises that have an instruction to use weights can be done just as easily without, at least to start with. As you exercise, pace yourself throughout and then finish as slowly as you began. If you feel faint or dizzy or out of breath at any time, stop immediately—you might be doing too much, too soon.

WHAT DO I NEED?

You do not need to buy any special clothing or equipment, unless you want to. Always dress in comfortable clothing that allows you to move, and make sure you are sufficiently warm, particularly when stretching out after any vigorous exercise.

Buy hand and leg weights if you wish (see pp22–23), or make do with items that you have around the house—cans of baked beans or soup can substitute for hand weights, as can plastic milk cartons (these give you the option of deciding how full, and therefore how heavy, you want them to be). Leg weights can be made from plastic bags filled with dried peas or beans. A towel or scarf will substitute very well for a stretchy exercise band, where necessary.

PLANNING YOUR TIME

If you're a beginner, start with two workouts per week of around 20 minutes, until you feel ready to build up to 30 minutes. You will be amazed at the results that a few regular sessions will have on your energy levels and overall feeling of well-being.

Choose a time of day to exercise that suits you and be prepared to change it, if the need arises. If you don't know what time of day suits you, then try exercising at different times. Many people like exercising in the morning, particularly if they are able to slot it in as part of their regular morning routine.

Remember to take it easy when you start exercising, and don't do more than feels comfortable—you will soon be fit enough to increase the pace.

maintaining a fitness regime

Beginning a new exercise plan is easy—keeping it going is much more challenging. You will need to learn how to keep yourself motivated and stay positive. If you are unhappy or bored with your fitness routine, then change it. Remember, you will only stick to something that is enjoyable for you.

There are many techniques that can help you feel more motivated, for example planning your exercise sessions in advance and putting them into your diary in the same way that you would any other appointment; keeping an exercise diary or journal in which you log each session and can easily monitor the progress you are making (see page 63); changing or varying your exercise routine regularly to make sure that you don't get bored. Try giving yourself specific daily and weekly "fitness" goals. These can be anything you like (a 20-minute run, or increasing your exercise repetitions from 10 to 15) but always make sure that your goals are easily within your reach.

Be patient with yourself and remember that it takes around 30 to 60 days to establish any new routine (such as a system of regular exercise). There will be times when you will feel that the last thing you want to do is go to the gym or get on with your exercises. At such times, acknowledge the feeling but insist to yourself that it is essential for you to do at least some daily exercise or activity—maybe 15 minutes instead of your usual 45, or half a mile instead of 2 miles. You will usually find that once

Give yourself credit. Recognize your achievements, however small, and congratulate yourself for having achieved them.

Listen to your body. If you are tired or feeling under par, ease up on your program, but do try to do some activity (such as going for a walk) each day.

ABOVE *If your body is telling you that it's not up to your full exercise program, try to take a daily walk until you feel fit again.*

you start you will be happy to carry on and meet your usual targets. But if you don't, or really can't find the time for any reason, don't worry—the most important thing is to make sure that you do some kind of activity every day, to keep yourself in exercise mode.

TRAINING WITH A FRIEND

Teaming up with a "fitness friend", someone who will train with you, is an excellent way to stay motivated, since it reduces the temptation to miss any of your workout sessions and can also encourage you to push yourself a little further. Naturally you will need to decide upon a routine that is acceptable to both of you. If you are unable to find a friend to train with, enlist the help of someone who is willing to act as your support— essentially someone who you "report" to, rather like signing in. At first, check in with them every day, then, as you begin to settle into a routine and get more into the habit of exercising, gradually drop the contact to a weekly check in.

ABOVE *Skipping is a great form of exercise, requiring only you, your skipping rope and a very small amount of space.*

LEFT *Exercise needn't be unsociable— choose an activity that enables you to spend time with the family, too.*

Plan some active fun outings for you and your loved ones— rollerblading, ice–skating, a family softball game, tennis or a bicycle ride.

If you really can't make your exercise "appointment" then rearrange your session immediately and substitute with some other activity: walk somewhere instead of driving, or put some music on and dance to three of your favorite tracks.

fitness for people over 55

It's never too early or too late to start exercising. Whether you are eight years old or 80, being fit and active will greatly improve your quality of life and help you stay and feel as young and healthy as possible.

There is no reason why you shouldn't be able to continue doing the same kinds of activities in your 50s as you did in your 20s, 30s and 40s. Indeed cardiovascular exercise and strength training is essential at this stage of your life. Many people complain of stiffness and loss of flexibility once they reach their mid-50s, so, if you are not doing so already, consider adding an activity that encourages flexibility, balance and muscle control—such as yoga, Pilates or tai chi.

Combining exercise with social activity—and possibly also a new challenge—is an excellent idea: join a dance class (ballet, ballroom or latin), take some figure-skating lessons, or even enroll at the local golf club. Swimming, walking, cycling and tennis are also excellent forms of exercise to keep you active and mobile.

If you are starting an exercise program for the first time, remember to work slowly and steadily and avoid pushing yourself too hard to begin with. If you start to feel any discomfort or find yourself getting over-tired, stop immediately.

Check with your doctor before undertaking any new fitness routine.

Don't worry about being unfit— learn to take each day as it comes. Think of your fitness routine as a journey, not a destination, and focus your attention on the next step of that journey.

USING HAND AND LEG WEIGHTS
Many exercises require you to use hand or leg weights. If you are using weights for the first time, again start slowly using either very light weights (2lbs/1kg, gradually building to 5lbs/2.5kg or 3kg), or use none at all until your strength has developed.

ABOVE *An activity that promotes flexibility will help to head off any stiffness you may experience at this age.*

UPPER BODY RELAXER

This exercise is great for releasing tension and stiffness and improving flexibility in the neck, shoulder and back areas.

Sit on the floor with your legs crossed. Contract your abdominals and lengthen up through the spine. Place your right hand on the floor and lower your right ear toward your right shoulder. Hold for 3 or 4 breaths, trying to increase the stretch with each outbreath. Inhale and roll your head slowly forward, taking your chin to your chest, then exhale and roll your head around to the left. Again take 3 or 4 breaths as you work to take your left ear to your left shoulder. Release and come up to center, then repeat in the opposite direction. Repeat the sequence 3–5 times.

your fitness plan

For exercise to have any real, lasting effect, it needs to become as much a part of your daily routine as cleaning your teeth. Only an ongoing commitment to a regular routine of exercise will bring about lasting, positive changes to your level of fitness.

GETTING INTO THE HABIT

Instead of deciding whether you should work out, be more positive and try asking yourself when you will work out. If you find that other areas of your life are starting to interfere with your fitness routine, be determined—refuse to give in and allow yourself to be pulled off-course, and definitely do not use those other areas as an excuse to neglect your program. Find ways to create clear boundaries to protect your new fitness schedule (for example, unplug the phone, turn off your cellphone, explain to other family members that you are not to be interrupted for the duration of your routine, and even lock or obstruct the door, if necessary).

The best exercises are the ones you do. Any exercise is good if it is done correctly, consistently and regularly.

Never be tempted to carry or wear hand or leg weights when out walking or running, or when doing activities around the house. Not only will they slow you down and therefore counteract any good effect that wearing them might give you, but they will change the way that you move, risking putting your body out of alignment and causing injury.

WHEN IS THE BEST TIME TO EXERCISE?

There are different ideas as to when is the best time to exercise. Some think that exercise should be done in the evening when the muscles are warmed up from the day's activities, some say that the morning is the optimum exercise time, and others maintain that standing exercises should be done in the morning and horizontal exercises in the evening... However, the best time is really the one that works for you and fits most easily into your schedule. Perhaps a relaxing evening session to help you unwind suits you, or maybe you would prefer an energizing early-morning regime to start your day?

PENCIL POINTING

This simple exercise is good for stretching the spine, lifting the ribcage and toning the waistline. It will also improve your posture and can even help pull you to your full height. Stand against a wall, with a pencil in your right hand. Reach up as high as you can and make a small pencil mark on the wall. Release and then repeat with your left hand. Practice this move every morning and evening. At the end of 20–30 days you will find that the marks will have moved up 1–3ins (2–6cms)!

STRETCHING AND STRENGTHENING

The exercises described in this book are made up of a mixture of stretching and strengthening moves. Several of the strengthening moves are described using light weights, but you can equally do them without weights, if you prefer. Going through the first set of repetitions of any moves without using weights is an excellent way to warm yourself up in preparation for the more intensive variation with the weights.

As a general rule, it is good to start with 2lb (1kg) weights, for both men and women, with men gradually increasing to 10–15lbs (5–8kg) and women increasing to 3–10lbs (2.5–5kg). Never push yourself too far, though, since you will risk strain or injury if you do so. You will benefit much more by working each move precisely and correctly at a lower level than by rushing to advance too quickly and doing the move inaccurately.

MEN AND WOMEN

Essentially there is little difference in approach to exercise for the two sexes. Women tend to be more flexible, while men tend to be stronger. This means that women will almost always require lighter weights than men. Some men prefer to build more muscle, while many women seek a longer, leaner look. However, both men and women benefit from developing strength, stamina, flexibility and muscle control, so on the whole the exercises for both will be identical. Women need to be careful not to push themselves to attempt any exercise that is actually too far beyond their current capabilities, while men can benefit enormously from making sure they always include some stretching in their exercise routine.

INJURY

Women do tend to be more prone to knee trouble than men, largely because of their wider pelvises, more supple joints and weaker hamstrings. Men's potential lack of flexibility can put them in danger of breaking bones more easily.

COMPETITION

Try to curb any inappropriate competitive tendencies you might have. On your exercise program the only person you need to compete with is yourself. Do not be tempted to make comparisons with other people around you and the progress that they appear to be making. Focus on your own goals, discover your own boundaries

and gradually work at pushing yourself just that little bit further—listening to your body will help to determine the best pace for you. Most of all, be kind to yourself and proud for the steps you have already taken. And remember, there is always time for improvement.

RIGHT Holding weights as you carry out the exercises will really help to increase your strength, although the exercises are still very effective without weights if you prefer not to use them. Start with light weights and progress gradually to heavier ones.

Walking is one of the best exercises, and is suitable for every individual. When taking up a fitness regime for the first time, taking short (20–30 minute) brisk walks, every day if possible, will be extremely beneficial because it gives a gentle workout to your entire body. If you enjoy walking and would like it to become a major part of your exercise, you might consider buying a pedometer, which will monitor the number of steps you take. Aim to add 500 per week to your walking sessions.

warming up and cooling down

A simple warm up is essential to any exercise program and should never be avoided since it allows you to stretch and mobilize the body gently in preparation for the more demanding exercises to come. A cooling-down period at the end will help avoid muscle strain or injury.

ROLLING DOWN

Stand with your feet hip-width apart, arms by your sides. Relax your shoulders. Contract your abdominal (stomach) muscles, exhale, then drop your head forward and start rolling slowly down through the spine, aiming the crown of your head down to your toes. Inhale as you roll slowly back up through the spine, starting at the tailbone and raising your head up last. Repeat 3–5 times.

Rolling down is excellent for increasing flexibility in the spine, reducing neck and shoulder tension and getting your energy flowing.

SHOULDER SHRUGS

You can use the same moves for both warming up and cooling down. Avoid rushing through them at the end of your session though—take the time to go through them slowly and carefully.

BALANCE

Stand with your feet hip-width apart, arms by your sides. Soften (slightly bend) your knees and relax your shoulders. Focus your eyes straight in front of you. Contract your abdominals and exhale as you rise slowly up onto your toes (avoid letting your ankles collapse out to the sides). Breathe in and hold for a few seconds, then exhale as you roll back down to the floor, trying to stay tall and keep the length in your spine. Repeat 5 times to start with, gradually increasing to 10.

Stand with your feet hip-width apart and inhale as you raise your shoulders up as high as you can. Hold for 2 seconds, then exhale as you drop them down again. Repeat 10 times.

SHOULDER CIRCLES

CHEST OPENER

Keeping your arms relaxed, raise your shoulders, then circle them forward 5–10 times and back 5–10 times. Finally, repeat the sequence, trying to circle your shoulders in opposite directions.

Place your hands on your hips, drop your shoulders, then pull your shoulder blades together and take your elbows back toward each other as far as possible to strengthen the back and stretch out the chest area.

HAMSTRING STRETCH (STANDING)

If you suffer from tight hamstrings, bend your knees slightly as you do this move. The important element is to work on warming up and mobilizing the spine.

Take a big step forward with your right foot, keeping your feet parallel. Hold on to a solid surface to help you balance, if necessary. Slowly bend your right knee and straighten your back leg, keeping your heel on the floor and creating a stretch through your hamstring muscle. Hold for 10 seconds then release. Repeat 3–5 times, then change legs and repeat on the other side. Ease yourself gently into this stretch, particularly if you suffer from any tightness here.

breathing and posture

Good posture and breathing are essential to our feeling of well-being and our ability to function properly. Taking the time to correct our posture and breathing at the start of any exercise routine brings our attention back into our bodies and helps us think more clearly, perform more efficiently and feel energized and more alive.

RHYTHMIC BREATHING

1 Lie on your back, arms at your sides, knees raised, feet flat on the floor hip-width apart. Inhale.

2 Exhale and contract your abdominals, raising your shoulders upward away from the floor and allowing your arms to lift. Inhale. Keeping the abdominals contracted, breathe out in 5 short breaths and "pulse" with your hands (pressing your palms slightly down toward the floor with each outbreath). Avoid hunching your shoulders—keep them dropped down, away from your ears. Release and lower back to the starting position. Repeat the sequence 5 times, gradually increasing the number of pulses to 10 then 20 for each repetition. Once you are able to hold the abdominal contraction and control the breathing for 20 pulses at a time, you are ready to move on, changing the sequence to 2 repetitions of 50 pulses each and then eventually to a single sequence of 100 pulses.

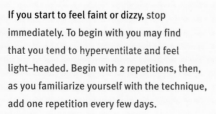
If you start to feel faint or dizzy, stop immediately. To begin with you may find that you tend to hyperventilate and feel light–headed. Begin with 2 repetitions, then, as you familiarize yourself with the technique, add one repetition every few days.

IMPROVING YOUR POSTURE

1 Stand with your feet parallel, hip-width apart, arms by your sides. Breathing normally, start at your feet and slowly take your attention up through your body, from your toes right to the top of your head. Notice any places of tension and try to relax and let go.

2 Relax your shoulders, allowing them to drop down away from your ears (avoid rounding them forward or forcing them back).

3 "Lengthen" through your spine and along your neck—imagine that there is a string running through your spinal cord: let it float up and out of the top of your head to the ceiling at one end, while dropping down through your tailbone to the floor at the other.

Avoid advancing too quickly: if you find that you are unable to sustain the abdominal control, return to an easier level in order to build up your strength.

This breathing exercise strengthens the abdominal muscles as it gently warms up the body.

THORACIC BREATHING

1 Sit or stand with your feet parallel, hip-width apart. Place your hands on your ribs, middle fingers touching. Drop your shoulders down away from your ears and draw your shoulder blades down into your back very slightly.

2 Keeping your chest relaxed, breathe into your lower ribcage and back. As you breathe, allow your ribcage to expand outward to the sides, back and front. Your fingertips will separate slightly (2–3ins/3–6cms) as you do so. Exhale and allow the ribcage to relax, bringing your hands back to the starting position. Repeat 5 times, trying to increase the movement of the ribs each time. Gradually increase the number of repetitions to 10 (or more, if you prefer).

20-day fitness program 1

Once you have warmed up you are ready to begin working the body a little harder. However, remember that it is much better to start slowly and build at your own pace than to push yourself too hard and become disheartened and possibly even risk muscle strain or injury.

When planning a new fitness regime, you will need to decide the format that will work best for you. Initially, in order to make any significant progress, you will need to set aside time to exercise at least every other day. Ideally, you should exercise a little each day, alternating between your cardiovascular exercises and activities (walking, running, cycling) one day and a stretching session the next. Experiment with the exercises over the next few pages and choose a few to do for each session (allow yourself 20–35 minutes to start with and gradually build to 35–45 minutes), either choosing ones to make sure that the body gets a thorough workout, or, for example, working your upper body one day and your lower the next. Just make sure that, over the course of the week, you have exercised all the different parts of the body equally.

An early-morning walk in the open air is an excellent way to start the day, taking plenty of oxygen into your system and getting your circulation flowing.

WALKING

One of the best exercises for giving your body an overall workout is, without question, walking. Not a stroll, of course, but a brisk walk (approximately 4 miles per hour) that raises your heart rate slightly and causes you to break into a slight sweat. Walk briskly for a minimum of 20 minutes at least once a week (twice is better, or even three times, if you can manage it).

STEP UPS

A diet high in fiber is thought to help prevent cancer of the colon and reduce the risk of furred-up arteries.

Calf raises stretch out the hamstring muscles at the back of the legs and are particularly good for men, who tend to be very tight in this area.

Contract your abdominals, stand up tall and step up onto the bottom stair (or a step) with your right foot followed by your left. Push down with the front foot to bring you up and just let the back leg come up to join it. Step back down, first with your right foot, then your left. Repeat, this time changing sides so that the left foot is leading. Repeat for 2–5 minutes, alternating the leading foot each time. Keep your abdominals contracted and get into a rhythm as you step.

CALF RAISES

Stand on the stair or step with your feet together, the balls of your feet on the edge of the stair. Drop the right heel down as far as you can, creating a stretch through the calf, while at the same time rising up onto the toes of the left foot. Release back to center, then drop the left heel and raise the right. Repeat 10–20 times using alternate feet. Repeat 10 more times, this time dropping and raising both heels together.

CURL UPS

Weak abdominal muscles can eventually result in backache. To strengthen your abdominals, try some curl ups. Lie on your back, with your knees bent, feet flat on the floor, and your arms crossed over your chest. Contract your abdominal muscles and curl up slowly until your shoulder blades are raised off the floor a little. Release back down. Repeat 5 times, then rest for 60 seconds. Repeat the sequence twice more.

REVERSE CURL UPS

Lie on your back with your knees bent and your heels as close as possible to your buttocks, feet flat on the floor. Contract your abdominals and slowly bring your knees toward your chest as far as possible, allowing your feet and your buttocks to rise up off the floor. Keeping the abdominals contracted, lower your knees back down. Repeat 5–10 times, increasing to 20.

WAIST TWIST

Stand with your legs hip-width apart, feet parallel. Raise your arms to just below shoulder level, with one forearm resting on top of the other. Keep your shoulders relaxed. Breathe out and twist around to the left, keeping your hips facing forward. Twist as far as you can without straining, then come back to center and repeat for the other side. Repeat 5–10 times.

PELVIC TILT

Lie on your back with your knees bent, feet flat on the floor. Contract your abdominals and tilt your pelvis upward very slightly, raising your tailbone an inch or two off the floor. Release. Repeat 10 times, keeping the abdominals contracted throughout. This a very small but effective exercise and is excellent for engaging the abdominals and releasing any tension in the lower back.

WALKING LUNGES

Step forward with your right leg, bending both knees and lowering yourself into a lunge position, making sure that your knee remains in line with your ankle. As you step back, raising yourself out of the lunge, immediately step forward with the other leg and lunge again. Repeat 10 times, gradually increasing to 20. Keep lengthening along your spine as you work (avoid leaning forward) and relax your shoulders.

HEEL KICKS

Lie face down with your face resting on your arms, your palms on the floor. Bend your right knee, bringing your foot up toward the ceiling, but keeping your thigh resting on the floor. Inhale, contract the abdominals and exhale, kicking the right heel toward the right buttock. Kick once more, then lower as you bend the left knee and raise the left foot. Repeat 5–10 times on each side.

ARM CIRCLES

Stand with your feet hip-width apart. Raise your right arm up in front of you, then curve it up and over your head and back down and round in a big circle. Repeat for 5–10 circles, then reverse the direction. Repeat for the other side. Now circle both arms at the same time, first in one direction, then the other, 5 more times. Keep your shoulders relaxed throughout. You will need to make the circles much smaller when you work both arms together. Concentrate on making the circling movement as smooth and even as possible.

CAT

Kneel on the floor in a box position with your knees beneath your hips and your hands beneath your shoulders. Contract your abdominals, tuck your pelvis under, drop your chin to your chest and slowly arch your back up toward the ceiling like a cat. Release back to center then exhale and lift your tailbone and head upward while curving your body down toward the floor. Inhale and release. Repeat the sequence 5–10 times.

SIDE BENDS (STANDING)

Standing with your feet hip-width apart, raise your arms over your head, crossing your arms and grasping each elbow with the opposite hand. Contract your abdominals, keep your shoulders relaxed, lift up through the waist and slowly bend over to the right. Slowly return to centre and repeat on the other side. Repeat the sequence 10 times.

BICEPS CURLS

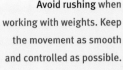
SINGLE ARM LIFTS

Still keeping your elbows down to your sides, bring both hands up to shoulder level. Slowly raise one hand straight up to the ceiling (avoid locking at the elbow), then slowly lower and repeat on the other side. Repeat for 10 lifts on each side. Do 2–3 sets of lifts, resting for 60 seconds between each set.

Try this exercise without weights and then add light weights once you are ready (women 2–5lbs/1–2.5kg, men 5–10lbs/ 2.5–5kg, people over 55 5lbs/1–2.5kg or nothing). Hold your elbows in to your waist, forearms out in front of you either holding weights or with hands made into fists, facing upward. Keeping your elbows in to your sides, slowly lift and lower each arm alternately 5–10 times on each side, then 5–10 times both arms together. Do 2–3 sets, resting for 60 seconds between each set.

CYCLING

Cycling is an excellent all-round exercise for firming and toning— particularly the legs, abdomen and buttocks—and for improving strength and stamina. A bicycle ride in the open air can also be an excellent mood lifter. If you don't own a bicycle, or if cycling is impractical for you and you do not have the option of an exercise bike, try this exercise instead, which has the added advantage of also working the upper body.

Lie on your back with your legs raised and your knees slightly bent, hands resting lightly behind your ears. Contract your abdominals and twist your body from side to side, bringing each knee towards your chest in a "pedalling" motion and touching that same knee with the opposite elbow as you do so. Start with 2 sets of 10 repetitions for each side, gradually increasing to 20. Repeat the sequence on alternate days.

BACK EXTENSION

Lie face down on the floor, hands directly below your face. Contract your abdominals and raise your chest an inch or two off the floor, keeping your forearms on the floor to support your body. Release. Repeat 5–10 times, rest for 60 seconds then repeat.

GLUTE SQUEEZE

Sit in a chair with your back straight. Contract your abdominals and squeeze your buttocks, holding for 3–5 counts, then release for 2. Repeat the sequence 10 times, gradually building to 20.

PILLOW SQUEEZE

Lie on your back with your knees bent, feet together, hands by your sides. Place a pillow between your knees, contract the abdominals and exhale, squeezing the inner thighs together for a count of 10 as you do so. Release. Repeat 10 times.

You can practice the glute squeeze at any time, wherever you are. For fast results and firmer buttocks, repeat the sequence 4–5 times throughout the day.

Although the back extension is an appropriate exercise for men and women alike, men (and stronger women) may wish to develop this move into a simple push–up.

PUSH–UP (OPTION 1)

Follow the instructions for the back extension, this time keeping your legs straight and raising your knees up off the floor. Slowly raise and lower 5–10 times, rest for 60 seconds, then repeat.

PUSH–UP (OPTION 2)

Repeat the above move, this time keeping your legs straight, raising your knees up off the floor and bringing yourself up onto your hands. Slowly raise and lower 5–10 times, keeping the movement slow and controlled. Rest for 60 seconds, then repeat.

LEG STRETCH

Lie on the floor with your knees raised. Slowly extend the right leg away from you along the ground, keeping your hips level and creating a stretch right through the leg. Inhale and bring the leg back to center.

Repeat 10 times, using alternate legs. Repeat the entire sequence, this time keeping the leg raised as you extend it out. Keep the abdominals contracted throughout.

20-day fitness program 2

By now you are 20 days into your fitness program and are probably starting to notice some changes. If you have been exercising regularly, your levels of fitness, strength, stamina and flexibility will have improved and you will be ready to move on to the next phase.

CARDIOVASCULAR EXERCISE

The aim with cardiovascular (aerobic) exercise is to raise your heart rate, get your muscles working, get your blood pumping and deepen your breathing. As a rough guide, many exercises use a system whereby you find your maximum heart rate (MHR) by taking 220bpm (beats per minute) and subtracting your age (220 – 40 = 180bpm). The aim is to spend a few minutes warming up with your heart rate at around half of your MHR rate, then to start increasing your heart rate until you reach around 80–85 percent of your MHR. For the last few minutes ease off a little and let your heart rate drop again as you cool down. Any exercise that raises your heart rate, increases your breathing and causes you to start to break into a sweat is a cardio-type exercise, for example running, brisk walking, cycling (either outdoors or using gym equipment), dancing or aerobics classes.

For the next 20 days, try to schedule in three "cardio" sessions per week (or at least two) — beginning and ending with some stretching, of course (see *Warming up and cooling down*, p26). Start with 15–20-minute sessions and gradually increase, by one minute at a time, aiming at a total time of 60–75 minutes per week. Switch between cardio sessions one day and strengthening and toning exercise sessions the next.

ABDOMINAL CURLS

Lie on your back with your knees raised, feet flat on the floor. Cross your arms over your chest. Contract your abdominals, exhale and curl your head, neck, then shoulders away from the floor slightly. Don't try to lift up too much, and use the abdominals to control the move. Inhale as you release back down to the floor, again keeping the abdominal control. Repeat 10 times, rest for 30 seconds, then repeat.

OBLIQUE CURLS

Starting from the same position as before, place your right hand behind your head, elbow pointing out to the side, and extend your left arm straight out at shoulder level. Contract your abdominals, exhale and curl your head, neck and shoulders away from the floor, aiming your left elbow toward your right knee. Keep contracting the abdominals as you inhale and lower yourself back down. Repeat 10 times, rest for 30 seconds then repeat. Repeat the sequence for the other side.

You may be thoroughly enjoying your new exercise routine, or perhaps the novelty is now starting to wear off and you are finding yourself struggling to discipline yourself to keep up your regular fitness sessions. Don't give up now! Recognize how well you are doing and be proud of what you have achieved so far. Ask for support from those you love to help encourage you to achieve your fitness goals.

PUSH–UP (WOMEN)

Lie face down on the floor, hands placed wide, outside your shoulders. Bring yourself up onto your hands and knees, arms straight. Contract your abdominals. Exhale and slowly lower your upper body to the floor, as you bend your arms, taking your elbows out to the sides. Inhale as you bring yourself back up, keeping the abdominals contracted and the back lengthened. Repeat 5–10 times, rest for 60 seconds then repeat.

Try to exercise every day for at least 30 minutes (with one day off a week to give your body a complete rest), still switching between cardio and stretching/toning on alternate days.

PUSH–UP (MEN)

Follow the instructions for the women's sequence (see p39), straightening your legs and raising your knees up off the floor. Keep your back in a straight line as you lower and raise, avoiding dropping at the hips.

(see p39)

VARIATION

IF YOU WANT MORE OF A CHALLENGE, bring your hands in closer together and/or elevate your feet (place them on a small box or stool, but make sure that it will not slip from under you).

RUNNING

PACE YOURSELF AND START SLOWLY, particularly if you have never run before and doubly so if this is the first time that you have undertaken a fitness plan. Always stretch before you start and stretch again for a few minutes at the end of your run. If you do not, you risk injury and will suffer from tight calves and hamstrings. To prepare for running, begin with several (3–6) brisk walking sessions. Now you are ready to instigate the "lamp post technique": begin by walking briskly from one lamp post to the next. Continue walking to the next lamp post, then pick up the pace and begin some easy jogging until the next one. Then slow down and walk again for 2 lamp posts, as before. Continue with this system for the duration of your "run" (15 minutes would be an ideal time to start with), walking for 2 lamp posts, jogging for 1, etc. As you develop and build up strength and stamina, change so that you are walking 1, running 1; then walking 1, running 2; walking 1, running 3, etc, until you are ready to cut walking altogether.

PLIÉS

Stand with your feet 2 feet apart, feet turned slightly outward (in a "10 to 2" position). Keeping your back straight and your shoulders in line with your hips (avoid leaning forward or back), squeeze your buttocks and slowly bend your legs, keeping your knees in line with your feet. Lower yourself as far as you can and hold for a slow count of 5. Release back to standing. Repeat 5 times, gradually increasing to 10 repetitions as you build up strength. If you need something to help you balance, hold on to a solid surface, but make sure that you keep your body in alignment.

SQUATS

This and the following few exercises can be done equally well with or without using handweights and are great for toning and strengthening hamstrings and buttocks.

Stand with your feet hip-width apart, legs straight, arms by your sides. Contract your abdominals, exhale and slowly bend your knees until you are in a squat position, leaning forward slightly as you lower and allowing your arms to drop forward in a relaxed position. Breathe in and slowly rise back to standing. Repeat 10 times, resting in between.

LUNGES

These are similar to the walking lunges exercise that appears in fitness plan 1, but this time using light handweights and stepping backward instead of forward.

Stand with your feet hip-width apart. Step backward with your right leg, bending both knees and lowering yourself into a lunge position, keeping your knees in line with your ankles as you lower your right knee toward the floor, keeping your heel raised. Return to the starting position and repeat for the other leg. Repeat 10 times, rest for 30 seconds then repeat.

ONE-ARM LIFT

You need only one handweight for this exercise: if you are not using weights, clench your hand into a loose fist. Stand with your feet hip-width apart, knees slightly bent, your left hand resting on your left knee or on the seat of a chair. Keeping your back as straight as possible, contract your abdominals and exhale as you slowly raise your right arm, pulling your shoulder blades in together and keeping your elbow into your waist. When you have raised as far as you can, straighten your right arm, extending it backward. Inhale as you bend your elbow and lower your arm. Repeat 10 times, rest for 30 seconds then repeat. Repeat for the left arm.

TRICEP EXTENSION

Sit with your feet flat on the ground and your back straight, shoulders dropped. Take a handweight in your right hand and straighten your arm up to the ceiling. Using your left hand to keep your upper arm steady, contract your abdominals and exhale as you slowly lower the weight down behind your head. Inhale and slowly raise your arm back up. Repeat 10 times, rest for 30 seconds then repeat. Switch hands and repeat the sequence for the other side.

REPEAT THE EXERCISE, holding the handweight in both hands, making sure that you keep your back straight, shoulders relaxed, abdominals contracted and upper arms stable as you lower and lift the handweight. Do 2 sets of 10 lifts, resting for 30 seconds between each set.

SEATED FLY

Sit on the edge of a chair with your feet hip-width apart, arms (a weight in each hand) hanging by your sides. Bend forward slightly. Contract your abdominals and drop your shoulders. Exhale and lift your arms straight out to the sides, pulling your shoulder blades in together. Release. Repeat 10 times, rest for 30 seconds, then repeat.

HALLELUJAH HANDSHAKE

This unusual exercise is excellent for reducing excess flesh at the backs of the upper arms. Sit or stand with your hands outstretched above you, abdominals contracted. Shake your hands, rotating them slightly at the wrists for as long as you can (10–15 seconds, or longer if possible), then drop your arms down by your sides and rest for 30 seconds. Repeat the sequence 3–5 times.

CHEST EXPANDER

Stand with your feet hip-width apart. Lace your fingers behind you and bring your arms up and over your head, bending forward with your body and keeping your legs and arms straight (knees soft, to protect your lower back). Stretch your arms forward as far as you can then slowly release (keeping your fingers laced), taking your arms back behind you and return to standing. Repeat 10–15 times.

Swimming is an excellent means of getting and staying fit. Nowadays many pools even offer water-fitness classes, including classes such as aqua fitness, aquaerobics, water Pilates, aqua combat and even aqua jogging. Check with your local pool to see what's available.

SIDEWAYS FLEX

Stand with your feet hip-width apart, arms above your head, hands pointing straight up to the ceiling. Contract the abdominals, exhale and extend your left arm over your head, lengthening up out of the waist and taking the body over to the right. Inhale as you return to center. Repeat for the other side. Repeat the sequence 10 times.

VARIATION

FOR A SLIGHTLY DIFFERENT STRETCH, or if this exercise is too difficult for you at this stage, place your left hand on your hip and curve your right arm over your head as you bend over to the left. Keep your back straight and your abdominals contracted.

BRIDGE

Lie on your back with your knees raised. Contract your abdominals and exhale, peeling your spine off the floor a short distance, starting with the tailbone. Inhale as you curl the spine back down onto the floor, then repeat several times more, gradually peeling a little more of your spine off the floor each time until you are resting on your shoulder area (4–5 times). Repeat several more times, to a total of 10–15 repeats. Control the entire move using the abdominals, keeping the movement slow and smooth throughout.

VARIATION

FOR PEOPLE OVER 55 or those who need to build strength in their abdominals. Lie on your back with both knees bent. Contract your abdominals, exhale and raise your right knee up toward your chest, keeping your leg bent. Inhale as you lower it back down. Repeat for the left leg. Repeat the sequence 10–20 times.

LEG RAISES

Lie on your back with your left knee bent and your right leg extended away from you, arms by your sides.

Contract your abdominals, exhale and slowly raise your right leg straight up to the ceiling. Inhale as you lower it,

keeping it an inch or two above the floor. Raise and lift 10–20 times on each side.

LEG LIFT SEQUENCE

To start with, practice all these exercises without ankle weights. Once you have built up strength in your legs, feel free to add light weights if you choose.

1 Lie on your left side with your left knee bent and your right leg stretched away from you. Rest your head on your left arm, bend your right elbow and place your right hand in front of your chest for support. Keeping your body steady, contract your abdominals and exhale as you raise your right leg an inch or two, then lengthen it out of the hip joint, stretching it away from you but keeping your hips stable. Inhale and release. Repeat 10 times.

2 Now, using the same motion (i.e. extending the leg away from you), raise and lower the leg for 2 sets of 10 times, resting for 30 seconds between each set.

3 Finally, alter your position so that your right knee is bent and resting on the floor and your left leg is extended away from you. Raise and lower the left leg. Repeat 20 times.

Change your position and repeat the entire sequence for the other side.

Do not get up quickly after you have been exercising lying down for any time, to avoid the possibility of dizziness.

20-day fitness program 3

Forty days into your routine and your metabolism will be revved up and raring to go. Remember to stay focused on achieving small, specific goals (for example, three weekly 45-minute exercise sessions) and to change your exercise formats so that you don't get bored.

Make activity an integral part of your life. Move as much as possible—walk, climb, cycle, lift, swim, stretch, exercise and play as often as you can. Switch sedentary activities for active ones, or add active elements to your sedentary activities (set a timer for each hour and get up and run up and down the stairs, lose the television remote control so that you have to get up every time you want to change the channel...). Also, learn to have fun by yourself as well as with others—buy yourself a skipping rope and skip in your back yard, and arrange to go for walks with your friends.

TOE BALANCE

Stand facing a wall, with your toes approximately 1ft (30cm) away from the wall. Place your hands lightly on the wall to help you balance, if necessary. Slowly raise your heels off the floor, rolling up through your feet onto your toes. Hold for a count of 3 and then slowly lower back down to the starting position. Repeat 5–10 times.

HIP OPENINGS

Lie on your left side with your head resting on your left arm. Place your right hand in front of your chest to stabilize you, and bend your knees, keeping your feet in line with your tailbone. Inhale, contract your abdominals and as you exhale raise the uppermost knee, keeping the feet together. Inhale and release the knee back down. Repeat 5–10 times on each side, completing 2 sets, resting for 30 seconds between each set. As you advance, lift the lower knee up from the ground too as you raise up.

This exercise should be avoided by women over 30 weeks pregnant.

SWIMMING

Position yourself in a "box" position on your hands and knees. Contract your abdominals and relax your shoulders. Extend your right leg and, at the same time, extend the opposite arm. Release and repeat for the other side. Repeat 10–20 times on each side.

VARIATION

FOR PEOPLE OVER 55, or anyone having difficulty with the above position. Follow the instructions for the move but position yourself so that you are lying on your front with your arms and legs extending away from you.

ARM OPENINGS

1 Lie on your back with your knees raised, a weight in each hand, your arms held straight up (elbows soft), palms facing inward. Contract your abdominals, exhale and open your arms slowly out to the sides, but not all the way to the floor. Inhale as you raise them back to center. Repeat 10–15 times, rest for 30 seconds, then repeat.

2 Hold your arms straight up, palms facing away from you. Follow the instructions for the above step, this time taking the left arm above your head and the right down toward the floor. Raise back to center, then take the left arm above your head and the right down to the floor.

Make time to exercise outdoors. Try to do at least 2 of your exercise sessions in the open air each week. Practice your breathing exercises (or even your regular daily workout) outdoors or by an open window, if you can, or take a short, brisk walk each day in the open air (in a pleasant, traffic-free environment).

WING STRETCH

Sit in a chair with your back supported and feet flat on the floor. Extend your arms out in front of you, palms downward, a weight in each hand. Contract your abdominals, exhale and take your arms out to the sides, keeping them at shoulder level, rotating your wrists so that your palms are facing forward. Make sure your shoulders stay as relaxed as possible. Inhale and bring your arms back to center. Repeat 10 times, rest for 30 seconds, then repeat.

CHEST PRESS

Lie on your back with your knees raised. Hold a weight in each hand at slightly above chest level, arms bent, palms facing away from you. Contract your abdominals, exhale and slowly raise your hands toward the ceiling, until your arms are fully extended above your chest. Inhale and slowly lower your arms. Repeat 10–15 times, rest for 30 seconds then repeat.

VARIATION

FOR PEOPLE OVER 55—ROTATED ARM CIRCLES. This deceptively simple exercise is excellent for toning the shoulders and the upper arms and opening out the chest. Raise your arms straight out to the sides at shoulder level, palms facing upward. Relax your shoulders and circle your hands slowly forward 20 times then back 20, making the circles about the size of a coconut. Rest for 30 seconds and repeat.

WALKING LEGS (SCISSORS)

Lie on your back with your arms by your sides, legs extended straight up. Contract your abdominals and "walk" in the air with your legs, taking one leg up toward your head and the other down toward the ground. Make the movements quite small to begin with; then, as you build up strength, start to take the legs lower, but make sure that you are able to keep the abdominal contraction as you move—if you start to lose it, you've gone too far.

SPINE TWISTS

Sit on the floor with your knees bent and your feet flat on the ground. Hold your arms straight out at shoulder level. Lower your upper body back slightly to an angle of approximately 45° (if you feel any pressure in your lower back, raise yourself up slightly). Slowly twist from side to side, 10–15 times on each side, bringing your arms across in front of you as you do so, while keeping your body steady.

Feel free to dip into the previous 2 exercise plans—don't feel that you must stick only with the exercises given in this section. The important thing is to make sure that you work the different muscles of your body evenly, either focusing on various parts of the body in different sessions, or using a balanced selection each time.

REVERSE ARM LIFT

Stand with your feet hip-width apart, knees slightly bent, a weight in each hand. Contract your abdominals and lean forward, keeping your back straight. Exhale and slowly raise both elbows up and back as far as you can, drawing your shoulder blades together, then straighten your elbows to extend your arms backward. Keep your shoulders down away from your ears. Inhale as you bend your elbows and bring your arms back to the starting position. Repeat 10 times, rest for 30 seconds then repeat.

REVERSE FLY LIFT

Stand with your feet hip-width apart, knees slightly bent. Contract your abdominals, keeping your spine straight, so that your back is roughly parallel to the floor. Exhale and slowly lift your arms out to the sides at shoulder height, elbows soft. Inhale and lower, controlling the move. Repeat 10 times, rest for 30 seconds then repeat.

LEG CIRCLES

Lie on your back with your knees bent, arms by your sides. Extend your right leg up toward the ceiling (the higher your leg the easier this exercise will be: lower your leg toward the floor for a more challenging exercise). Contract the abdominals, exhale and draw 5–10 small circles with your foot, first in one direction, then the other. As you circle, lengthen the leg out of the hip joint, keeping the opposite leg steady throughout. Repeat for the other leg. Repeat the entire sequence 3–5 times.

VARIATION

FOR PEOPLE OVER 55 OR WANTING A SLIGHTLY EASIER OPTION TO THE LEG CIRCLES EXERCISE.

Follow the instructions for the move (see p50, opposite) but keep your right (raised) leg bent, so that the knee is at a right-angle, with the shin parallel to the floor. Place the fingertips of your right hand on your right knee to guide you and circle the knee instead of the foot.

DOUBLE-LEG LIFT

Lie on your right side with your head resting on your right arm, legs extended away from you, knees and feet together. Contract your abdominals, exhale and raise your legs, keeping your hips level and your waist lifted away from the floor. Inhale as you release back down, but do not take your legs all the way to the floor. Lower and lift 10–20 times, rest for 30 seconds then repeat. Repeat for the other side.

IDEAS FOR ACTIVITIES

NOW THAT YOU ARE BECOMING more and more active you might like to think of taking up an activity (or several). Don't get caught up in what you think you "ought" to do, though: remember, it is supposed to be fun, so choose something that inspires you. Maybe there's something you've always longed to do but never previously had the opportunity? Now's your chance—remember, it's never too late...

Abseiling	Football	Soccer
Aerobics	Frisbee	Squash
Baseball, softball	Golf	Swimming
Basketball	Hang gliding	Synchronized swimming
Bellydancing	Hiking	Tai chi
Body combat	Horseriding	Tennis
Boxing	Ice–skating	Trampolining
Cheerleading	Martial arts – karate, tai quando,	Volleyball
Circus skills	aikido...	Water fitness – aquaerobics, aqua
Dance – ballet, line dancing, Latin,	Pilates	fitness, diving...
ballroom, jive, hip-hop, street,	Racketball	Watersports – sailing, water-skiing,
body popping, jazz...	Rock climbing	bodysurfing, scuba diving...
Dance combat	Skiing	Yoga

If you have been exercising regularly for 30 minutes each day, you will now be ready to up the duration of your sessions, presuming you have time within your schedule, of course. This does not mean that you would need to do a 45–60-minute session every day—it is equally effective to break your exercise program into different sections of 10–20 minutes, if that works better for you.

WALL SQUATS

Stand with your back against a wall or door with your feet parallel, hip-width apart, 1ft from the wall. Slowly slide down the wall to a sitting position, with your knees at right-angles, and hold for a slow count of 10. Release and slide back up to standing. Repeat 5 times. As you build up your strength, gradually increase the count to 20 and then, if possible, to 30.

LUNGE STRETCH

Stand with your feet as wide apart as possible, keep your left foot pointing forward, and turn your body to the right, moving your right foot so that it points to the side. Lower and lunge slowly forwards over your right foot as far as you can, aiming for your knee to be at a right-angle. Keep your left leg straight but avoid locking your knee. Return to center and repeat for the other side. Repeat 5 times on each side. Stop immediately if you feel any strain in either of your knees.

PRAYER POSE

Kneel on all fours, with your knees directly below your hips and your hands below your shoulders. Lower yourself back, sitting back on your heels with your arms stretched out in front of you. Rest your forehead on the floor. Hold for 5 to 10 breaths (or longer if you prefer), using each out breath to let go of a little more tension.

DOWNWARD DOG

Position yourself with your hands and feet on the floor, feet hip-width apart and hands shoulder-width apart, fingers spread wide. Lean your weight forward onto your hands slightly and press your heels to the floor to a count of 5, keeping your legs straight. Release. Repeat 10 times.

HAMSTRING STRETCH

Lie on your back with your knees raised, feet flat on the floor. Raise your right knee, extending your leg up toward the ceiling. Place your hands around your right thigh, contract your abdominals, exhale and gently draw the thigh in toward your chest. Inhale and release. Repeat 10 times, trying to increase the stretch with each out breath. Lower the right leg. Repeat for the left leg.

quick reference exercise plans

Alternate these suggested exercise routines with your cardio workouts—brisk walking, running and cycling. The time you have available will determine the number of exercises you will be able to perform. Try to cover all the exercises each week, but be creative and adapt the routines as you wish.

Always begin each routine with a short warm up and take a few minutes to stretch your muscles at the end of your session.

WARMING UP AND COOLING DOWN

rolling down	shoulder circles
balance	chest opener
shoulder shrugs	hamstring stretch

20-DAY EXERCISE PLAN 1

ROUTINE 1	ROUTINE 2	ROUTINE 3	ROUTINE 4
step ups	step ups	calf raises	step ups
calf raises	calf raises	curl ups	curl ups
curl ups	curl ups	reverse curl ups	reverse curl ups
pelvic tilt	pelvic tilt	pelvic tilt	waist twist
waist twist	waist twist	cat	walking lunges
heel kicks	heel kicks	arm circles	heel kicks
cat	arm circles	biceps curls	back extension
arm circles	biceps curls	single arm lifts	leg stretch
back extension	back extension	cycling	glute squeeze
glute squeeze	leg stretch	glute squeeze	pillow squeeze
pillow squeeze	pillow squeeze	hamstring stretch	hamstring stretch

20-DAY EXERCISE PLAN 2

ROUTINE 1	ROUTINE 2	ROUTINE 3	ROUTINE 4
abdominal curls	abdominal curls	abdominal curls	push up
oblique curls	oblique curls	oblique curls	pliés
push up	squats	push–up	lunges
pliés	lunges	pliés	squats
squats	one-arm lift	squats	one-arm lift
lunges	seated fly	tricep extension	seated fly
one-arm lift	tricep extension	bridge	hallelujah handshake
sideways flex	hallelujah handshake	sideways flex	chest expander
bridge	chest expander	leg raises	sideways flex
leg raises	leg lift sequence	leg lift sequence	bridge

20-DAY EXERCISE PLAN 3

ROUTINE 1	ROUTINE 2	ROUTINE 3	ROUTINE 4
toe balance	toe balance	hip openings	hip openings
hip openings	swimming	arm openings	swimming
swimming	wing stretch	walking legs	wing stretch
arm openings	chest press	spine twists	chest press
walking legs	spine twists	reverse arm lift	walking legs
spine twists	reverse arm lift	reverse fly lift	lunge stretch
leg circles	reverse fly lift	leg circles	wall squats
lunge stretch	double-leg lift	double-leg lift	downward dog
downward dog	hamstring stretch	prayer pose	hamstring stretch

keeping track of your progress

Keeping track of your progress can help you to stay focused on your fitness plan and motivated over the longer term. A positive and effective way of doing this is to learn to act as your own personal trainer.

Personal trainers are expert at keeping their clients motivated, pushing them further, helping them realize their full potential and giving them the confidence to achieve what they would never have thought possible. Here are a few pointers to show how you can achieve this for yourself.

FINDING TIME

You do not need hours of free time in order to commit to a regular fitness routine. If necessary, short bursts of activity can be sufficient to keep you active and fit. Be creative in finding ways to establish exercise sessions within your schedule, no matter how busy you are. Plan your sessions, but also allow yourself alternatives—plan A on a particular day could be a session in the gym with 35 minutes on the treadmill, followed by 20 minutes of toning exercises on the resistance machines;

while plan B, on the other hand, could be a 15-minute walk to your afternoon meeting, followed by a 10-minute stretching session when you get home.

BE READY FOR ANYTHING

If you can, get into the habit of always carrying some gym clothes or a pair of sneakers with you. That way you will always be ready to exercise, if the opportunity arises. For example, if you miss your train, instead of grabbing a coffee, put on your sneakers and go for a walk. On very busy days where you really have no space for any dedicated exercise time, rearrange one of your more informal meetings or your lunch appointment so that you can walk as you talk.

RING THE CHANGES

Avoid getting bored or stuck in a rut by constantly making changes to your exercise routine—alter the order in which you carry out your exercises, vary the length of your sessions, replace some of the exercises entirely. It is much more interesting to do slightly different exercises each time—sticking to exactly the same routine all the time is bound to result in boredom. Changing your routine will also help you to stay focused and will therefore encourage you to keep up the intensity of your workout.

Keeping an exercise journal can be a very helpful way of monitoring your progress. It's entirely up to you how you organize it. It could be totally factual, with dates, durations and the type of exercises you performed, or you may choose to keep a record of your physical state and any fluctuations or changes, or even make notes on how you feel before, during and after your sessions.

Acknowledge your achievements, however small, and be proud of yourself for attaining them.

Working from your abdominal "core" when you exercise, instead of merely moving your limbs, will allow you to exercise more effectively, improve your overall flexibility, strength and muscle control and reduce the risk of strain or injury, particularly to your lower back.

The advantage of working on a treadmill is that you can change both the speed and the incline, enabling you to work very hard or take it easy, depending on how you feel.

dealing with problem areas

A regular and varied fitness routine is undoubtedly the best way to get our bodies into prime condition and keep them that way. However, many of us have specific "problem" areas that we are unhappy with and are eager to focus on changing. Here are some ideas to inspire you.

When we commit ourselves to a regular exercise plan we usually find that, over time, our bodies naturally come into balance and those once troublesome spots disappear. When seeking to make lasting changes there are various points that we need to remember. Be patient—lasting changes don't happen overnight, so don't get disheartened if you don't see immediate results. Be consistent—it's no good just doing exercises once or twice and expecting to see a change. Be realistic— accept and appreciate yourself the way you are; don't be fooled into a false media image of how you think you should be (be it muscular hulk or slender waif).

You will need to control your diet and eat nutritious, well-balanced meals—it's no good tucking into a large helping of fries after every workout.

LEGS AND THIGHS

If you want to firm and tone your legs, make sure you do some kind of leg exercise every day. Some of the best moves for toning your thighs are squats (p41), pliés (p41), lunges (pp33 and 42) and leg lifts (with or without weights, p45). Combine these with a cardio workout (for example running, cycling, brisk walking). To firm your buttocks, add in the bridge (p44) and the glute squeeze (p36).

WAIST AND STOMACH

To tone your stomach area and slim your waistline, focus on exercises both for the abdominals and the obliques (the muscles that run across the abdominal area). Some good exercises are abdominal curls (p38) and oblique curls (p39), sideways flex (p44), waist twist (p33), step ups (p31), leg lifts (p45) and leg circles (p50). A very easy but effective exercise that can be done anywhere and at any time is simply to pull your navel in towards your spine, then hold for a few seconds and release. Do 5 repetitions of this whenever you remember—every hour throughout the day if possible.

LEG LIFTS *p45*

WALKING LUNGES *p33*   **SQUATS** *p41*

BUTTOCK WALK

This is an easy exercise to help trim your bottom.

Sit on the floor with your legs straight out in front of you and hold your arms in front of you at just below shoulder height, forearms resting one on top of the other if you like. Contract your abdominals, sit up tall and "walk" forward on your bottom for 8 "steps" and then back for 8. Repeat 5–10 times. Practice this every day, if possible.

OBLIQUE CURLS *p39*

TRICEP EXTENSION *p43*

CHEST OPENER *p26*

ARMS AND UPPER BODY

Using free weights is an excellent way to tone and strengthen arms and upper body. Practice arm circles and lifts (pp34 and 35), chest press (p48), chest opener (p26), hallelujah handshake (p43), push up (pp39–40), biceps curls (p35) and tricep extension (p43).

If you want to change your shape, whether you're looking to get rid of a little extra flesh or build some serious muscle, you will need to include regular cardiovascular exercise in your program. To help burn fat all over your body, develop strength and stamina, and help build and define muscle, make sure you work up a sweat by running or cycling at least 3 times a week.

pregnancy

The best time to get fit is before you become pregnant, but it's never too late to start. If you are already pregnant, the most important thing for you to remember is to start slowly each time you exercise and then to finish your exercise session as slowly as you began.

Dramatic changes occur in a woman's body during pregnancy and just after childbirth—exercising can help your body to adapt to these changes and keep you in top form for a healthy birth.

Many women suffer from back pain during pregnancy because of the postural changes caused by the extra weight being carried in the front of the body. Exercising to strengthen the back and stretching to release any tension can greatly help to relieve this problem. During the first half of pregnancy, any exercise that helps strengthen the abdominal area, together with those that help improve breathing, posture and alignment, will be invaluable, for example balance (p25), various breathing exercises (pp28–29) and chest opener (p26).

Cat (p34) and downward dog (p53) are particularly good for strengthening the back, while step ups (p31), calf raises (p31), hamstring stretch (p27) and leg lifts (p45) will stimulate the circulation in the legs.

After the 30-week mark, avoid any leg movements that require you to extend the leg to the side, opening out the hip joint. Head and neck exercises (p21) and shoulder and arm circles (p26 and p34) will help release tension and improve posture.

Hormonal changes within the body cause the ligaments to soften and the joints to become weaker and therefore high-impact activities, or those with intense jerky movements, are to be avoided as they risk causing damage to the joints.

After 30 weeks, when you are no longer able to lie on your back, try exercising lying on your side instead, using cushions to help support you.

An exercise that is highly recommended during pregnancy is the Kegel exercise, which can be done at any time, wherever you happen to be. Simply squeeze with the muscles of the pelvic floor, as if stopping the flow of urine, and hold for a few seconds. Repeat throughout the day, aiming at holding the squeeze for 10 seconds at a time.

BELOW *Walking is good exercise even when you are heavily pregnant, as it keeps the circulation moving.*

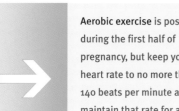

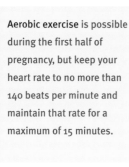

Consult your doctor before entering into any new fitness program during pregnancy or soon after childbirth.

Aerobic exercise is possible during the first half of pregnancy, but keep your heart rate to no more than 140 beats per minute and maintain that rate for a maximum of 15 minutes.

Exercises such as the hamstring stretch, which stimulate circulation in the legs, are very beneficial during pregnancy. Supporting the front foot helps you to ease gently into the stretch.

If you experience any pain, discomfort or tiredness while exercising, stop immediately.

EXERCISES TO AVOID DURING PREGNANCY

Intense stretching or resistance exercises using weights

Scuba diving, water-skiing, diving and jumping into pools, or any other high-impact exercise with rapid, jerky movements

Sprinting

Cycling in racing position

Any contact sports (football, wrestling)

Any strenuous exercise that raises your heartbeat above 140 beats per minute

In later pregnancy (from 30 weeks onward), avoid exercising lying on your back, or movements that require you to extend the hip joints (e.g. squats)

nutrition & fitness diaries

Use these blank templates to create personal nutrition and fitness diaries that will enable you to pinpoint your goals, keep track of your progress and stay motivated as you work through your chosen program. Use the comments/progress columns to record your motivation and energy levels, as well as your achievements.

NUTRITION DIARY

DATE	COMMENTS
BREAKFAST	
LUNCH	
DINNER	
SNACKS	
WATER	
OTHER DRINKS	

FITNESS DIARY

1 MONTHLY GOAL:

2 WEEKLY GOAL:

3 DAILY GOAL:

DATE						
AEROBIC EXERCISE	TIME	REPS	OTHER EXERCISE	TIME	REPS	PROGRESS

index

picture credits

CORBIS: pp 4 Mike Chew, 7 Steve Prezant, 13 Steve Prezant,

14 Lou Chardonnay, 15 Michael Keller, 20 Chuck Savage,

30 Jim Cummins, 57 Raoul Minsart, 60 Tom Stewart.